A Gravedigger's Tales

by

Ian Shipley

Grosvenor House
Publishing Limited

This book is published by
Grosvenor House Publishing Ltd
28-30 High Street, Guildford, Surrey, GU1 3HY.
www.grosvenorhousepublishing.co.uk

A CIP record for this book
is available from the British Library

ISBN 978-1-907211-66-9

Dedication

To my wife, Alison

To all my family

With thanks to Viv and Boz Mugabe

Contents

CHAPTER 1

A life's work

It does not feel like 27 years since I first walked through the gates of Newark Cemetery. I have spent so much of my life working there that it is now as familiar to me as my own back garden. In that time I have completed many tasks, but for the life of me I cannot explain why I do what I do. Yet I'm still as passionate now as I was on the day of my first dig, and I have never once contemplated moving on or trying something new. I have always been at ease with all aspects of cemetery work, so perhaps my vocation in life was to be a gravedigger.

I've always believed Newark Cemetery to be one of the best cared-for in Nottinghamshire. Spring and early summer is when the graveyard is at its finest. From late February the first row on either side of the main avenue suddenly bursts into life with an abundance of colour, as a carpet of purple and white crocuses seemingly emerge from out of nowhere. It's a spectacular sight and one that should not be missed.

In my early years I do recall that there were just as many yellow and golden crocuses as there are purple and white today, but unfortunately squirrels developed quite a liking for them and devoured the lot. Wherever you look there are eye-catching pockets of colour, as a wide range of plants and bulbs simultaneously come alive. The list of plants is vast but you can easily spot the likes of Meadow Buttercup, Primrose, Greater Stitchwort, Wild Garlic, Bluebell, Snowdrop, Winter Aconite, Crocus (mixed species), Narcissus (mixed species), Hyacinth, Tulip, Periwinkle, Cyclamen, Celandine, Daisy and - not forgetting my favourite - Foxglove. In recent years I have also seen the poisonous Ragwort and Deadly Nightshade.

The old timers must be credited for the majority of the work done, though each generation of workers has duly left its individual mark. Over a ten year period, my colleagues and I planted literally thousands of bulbs, mainly daffodils, in order to continue what others had previously started. It was a back-breaking and time-consuming task, but the end results were well worth it. Wildflower areas were also recreated, and in later years these have been both added to and further developed.

When I first started working at Newark Cemetery, there was a rotating cycle of tasks which was completed annually. Gravedigging was always given priority, but starting in the spring the list would begin with the levelling and turfing of all graves. Perimeter fencing, including all gates, was painstakingly wire-brushed and painted, as were the public toilets. All flowerbeds and herbaceous borders were maintained, and jobs like sweeping the main drive, emptying the litter bins and war grave maintenance were done on a weekly basis. Grass cutting would not begin until after Easter, and not until the second week in June would the first row along the main avenue be cut back, allowing sufficient time for bulbs and plants to die back naturally.

Throughout the summer, assistance was given to the maintenance and watering of the town's hanging baskets. Rose beds were fertilised and hedges were trimmed while the grass grew long and often out of control. The onset of autumn saw a repeat of the grave-levelling programme. Bulbs and new trees were planted and time was always given to making good the Commonwealth war graves' section in time for All Souls and Remembrance Day. All benches were removed and stored before the mother-of-all chores began - leaf collecting. The winter months were slow and cold, though there was always plenty of grave digging to be done. In the intervening time we would refurbish all the wooden benches, as well as assisting with putting up the town's Christmas lights. For me, the one job that ulti-mately signalled the closing stages of winter and the coming of spring was the removal of Christmas holly wreaths. In most cases this would begin during the first week in February. This annual schedule was simple and easy to remember and it actually worked. Nothing was rushed and, as the old timers would say, 'Work to live, not live to work.'

In 1988 a flowerbed, measuring 50ft long by 10ft wide, was created on the west side of the Garden of Remem-brance and within it were built three memorial plinths. Planted with summer begonias, it became an immediate success - so much so that a similar-sized bed was produced on the opposite side. Eventually the two beds were extended to 150ft long and ran parallel to the main drive. In 2000 they were reduced in size and split into four separate beds, which still feature today. In their heyday 3,500 bedding plants were used and at the height of summer they looked superb. A whole variety of plants was used but it was Busy Lizzies that always came out tops. I believe they simply thrived on the vast amounts of leaves that were dug in year after year - they loved it! The two beds soon became the cemetery's leading feature and we were often complimented on their upkeep. However, I do recall a time when a passerby suddenly stopped and commented, 'One year's weeds equals seven years' seeds' and then cycled off.

As you enter Newark Cemetery via the main gates off London Road, you cannot fail to notice the many trees that grace the grounds. There are over 600 trees set within its 21 acres. The main central broad walk boasts 130 trees, all of which are lime and aged 100 years plus. Throughout the grounds a variety of species can be found, though traditional favourites like the Oak, Lime, Beech, Holly, Spruce, Horse Chestnut and Yew dominate the landscape. The Yew tree is a dominant feature in any cemetery or churchyard. Shrouded in myth and mystery, this tree is often referred to as the 'Death Tree'. The Yew is associated with immortality, regeneration and rebirth. It was often planted to ward off evil spirits, and often sprigs of yew were thrown into the grave, thus protecting the soul on its journey into the other world. The entire tree, including the wood, bark, needles and seed are poisonous. It is also believed that any cutting down or burning of yew would bring bad luck.

There is, however, one species of tree that can no longer be found in the cemetery and that is the Elm. One old timer told me that in years gone by there were many such trees and they were a prominent feature, but they had become diseased and had to be felled. I was told a story of one particular elm tree; it was a big tree, which had been cut down and removed from site using the cemetery's own donkey and cart. It was taken to a local wood-yard where it was sawn into planks. A local undertaker then made coffins from them and, within a short space of time, these coffins were buried in the cemetery. How about that for recycling!

CHAPTER 2

Sorrowful tales

One certainty in life is that at some point in time we will all die. When, where and how is undetermined, though when it does occur, we are never prepared. A pallbearer once said to me, 'Every time someone dies, your name gets closer to the top of the list.' I just hope it's a very long list!

The first time I gave death any real thought was in 1978, when two brothers died in tragic circumstances. The brothers, aged nine and 11, lived on our street and, although they were not well known to me, we did occasionally play football together. On Valentine's Day of that year the two boys went to skate on a frozen pond. Unaware of the danger, the brothers fell through the thin ice and sadly both drowned.

Every cemetery or churchyard has its own tales of woe and Newark Cemetery is no different. In the older section there are a couple of headstones that always catch my eye. The inscriptions read that their occupants were accidentally shot and accidentally poisoned. Each time I pass by them I can't help but wonder about the story surrounding their untimely deaths. In another grave are a mother and her three children, who all died in a house fire. You can only imagine the grief of such a tragic loss. So too, it could be said, of John and Mary Smith whose three children are buried in the grave of Joseph Smith (bank manager). Their only daughter, Lizzie Ann, was born in 1865, but died 14 weeks later. Son Percy was born in 1867, but died aged three weeks, and their third child, named John, was born in 1869 but died aged just 19 days. Although the mortality rate for children in the nineteenth century was high, you can't help but feel for the parents as this repeated loss must have been devastating.

One story with an unfortunate twist of fate is that of the heroic nurse, Ethel Harrison. Ethel, from Newark, was nursemaid to the three children of a Mr and Mrs Anderson of Chester. On December 7th, 1906 - while walking along the towpath of the Shropshire Union Canal - five-year-old Jimmy Anderson fell in. Ethel immediately jumped in and was able to hand the boy to another nurse. Unfortunately, however, Ethel was swept away to the middle of the canal, where she drowned. She was buried in Newark Cemetery and, as a tribute to her memory, the townsfolk of Newark paid for a memorial fountain, which was sited near gardens where London Road and Balderton Gate meet. In 2007 this memorial was restored and unveiled again; it is a fitting tribute to a brave lady.

In 1935, Frederick Nodder (44) moved from Sheffield to his new lodgings at 11 Thoresby Avenue, Newark (close to where the cemetery is extended to today). His stay was short term, but he was popular with his landlady's children (a Mrs Tinsley) and, by all accounts, they called him Uncle Fred. He was described as an ugly, brutish drunk who had an appalling hygiene problem. It was also said that he couldn't hold down a job. Fred was soon to move to East Retford, but kept no contact with the Tinsley family. On Tuesday, January 5th, 1937 ten-year-old Mona Tinsley did not come home from school. Police investigations soon revealed that Mona had been seen with Fred at Newark bus station. This he denied, but witnesses had seen them together and so he was arrested and charged with abduction. By March 1937, despite a massive search, Mona could not be found. The police were convinced that Nodder had murdered the girl but, without a body, the charge of murder could not be brought. At Nodder's trial, charged with abduction, Justice Swift sentenced him to seven years' imprisonment. On June 6th, 1937 the badly decomposed body of a little girl was found floating in water on the River Idle near Bawtry. It was Mona Tinsley and she had been strangled. At Nodder's second trial he was convicted of her murder and was sentenced to death. Fred was hanged at Lincoln Prison on Thursday, December 29th, 1937. Mona Tinsley was buried in Newark Cemetery.

There are a number of distinguished people buried in Newark Cemetery, and one of the best known is the historian of the area, Cornelius Brown. He was a journalist, editor of the Newark Advertiser and author of seven books, including the History of Newark Volumes 1 + 2, which took him 15 years to complete. Sadly, he was never to see his final work in print as he died just four days after finishing the final proofs. His grave can be found in the older part of the cemetery. Other bene-factors of Newark who are buried in the cemetery include Thomas Earp (brewer), Joseph Gilstrap (malt-ing), William H Cubley (artist), William Newzam Nicholson (agricultural implements) and the Cafferata family, who were the suppliers and manufacturers of plaster and bricks from which much of the town has been built.

From time to time I'm asked if I have ever dug a grave for anyone famous. The answer is no, well not in the celebrity sense. I have dug graves for a Polish ambassa-dor and for Sir Godfrey Hounsfield CBE, the inventor of the CT scanner. To date, this is as far as my celebrity gravedigging goes.

CHAPTER 3

End of an era

When I began my time at Newark Cemetery, the superintendent in charge was a man called Mr Tommy Tate.
He was extremely well respected and highly thought of.
He knew burial law, he knew his staff and, as a result, the
job ran like clockwork. His relationship with his team
developed into a tightly-linked bond and he welcomed no
outside interference. Like all the old timers he was traditional, firm but fair. He often said to me 'Pay attention to
the job and complete one task at a time, for there's always
tomorrow. Besides, the cemetery will still be here when
we're all dead, buried and gone.'. How true!

I first met Mr Tate in the spring of 1981 when the careers
office sent me for an interview for the position of
gravedigger. Even now I can quite clearly recall that
odious first meeting. Entering his office, he looked me up
and down and asked directly, 'What do you want?'
Nervously, I explained myself but it was immediately
apparent that Mr Tate was not at all interested in
anything I had to say, as he just sat quietly staring out of
his office window. When I had finished, there was a long
pause; an unsettling silence. Eventually he turned to me,

looked me in the eyes and bluntly stated, 'There is no job. I don't know why they have sent you. Besides, if there were, I'd never employ a skinny school leaver, as the work is far too physically demanding.' And with that he promptly dismissed me from his office. I was dumbfounded by his response, but never forgot his words. A year later I was to return for a second interview. I was apprehensive at the thought of meeting him again, but I fared much better as I was instantly offered the job. I was well pleased though I always wondered if he actually remembered me from our first meeting.

Mr Tate took great pride in how the cemetery looked. He had three passions - his roses, the war graves and, more importantly, his trees. How he loved his trees! And, no matter how much they needed it, he would not permit any to be pruned or cut back in any form. I have been told that in years gone by, during the summer months walking up the cemetery's main avenue was like walking in the dead of night because it was that dark.

Each August Tommy would take his annual two weeks leave. On one occasion, unknown to him, secret plans had been made to completely cut back all the trees. A man they called Farndon Bob had been drafted in to complete the work, which began the minute Tommy left. All the lime trees along the main avenue were cut and pruned with dramatic effect, thus changing the way the cemetery looked forever.

On Mr. Tate's return, I'm told, he blew his top; he was so angry that it was said he raged for weeks afterwards as he could not believe that anyone could have dared to go behind his back. What of Farndon Bob? Well, until that point he had been a frequent visitor to the cemetery and well known to all the staff. However Tommy was so outraged by what he had done that he banned him from ever entering the grounds of Newark Cemetery again.

Tommy Tate was superintendent at Newark Cemetery from 1961 to 1982. He took over from a Mr George Wiggins. After Tommy's death a tree was planted and a bench sited but, although he had always reserved himself a burial plot within the cemetery, he was cremated and his ashes returned to his home city of Leeds.

CHAPTER 4

21 silver Rolls Royces

I have personally witnessed some grand send-offs in my time, but this was a sight to be seen. Following behind a sleek-looking silver hearse, was a cortege of 21 identical Rolls Royces. It was nothing but impressive, but I couldn't help but wonder just where they had got all the matching cars. The deceased was a woman who had tragically died at a relatively young age. I was informed that she had been married to an extremely wealthy businessman. He in turn had made it known that no expense would be spared for his wife's funeral. Everything had to be in order and everyone stylishly presented, because he was burying his queen, the love of his life.

The grave - a double-depth reopener - was in an existing family plot in the older part of the cemetery. It was a difficult dig because of its size and the location in which it was sited. The solid oak casket meant having to dig a bigger-than-normal grave in an area not set out for this typ of burial. As graves at this time were hardly ever , I was worried that it might collapse. Fortunately the well knitted-together sand/gravel mixture was both sturdy and dry; nevertheless this meant little, because the dividing grave walls on either side were thin and unstable. On the day of the funeral I felt for the pallbearers, as it was not an easy carry to the graveside. One slip, trip or fall could have ruined a well-planned day, never mind a collapse. My fingers were crossed!

The cortege, in all its full splendour, stretched the entire length of the main drive. There were a lot of mourners and I recall joking to my colleague that M&S must have done a roaring trade in shirts and trousers, as all the men were dressed identically. The women too were elegantly presented and many wore flamboyant hats, like those worn at Ascot. Indeed, the whole funeral was perfectly co-ordinated.

Just moments after the mourners had gathered around the grave, the funeral director suddenly emerged from the crowd and began to walk briskly towards me. My heart missed a beat, as I honestly thought the grave had collapsed. The undertaker must have sensed what I was thinking as he smiled and said, 'Don't look so worried, everything's in order.' He then whispered quietly, 'The husband has asked if he could possibly borrow a shovel, as he wishes to partially backfill the grave himself.' Well, I wasn't going to argue with that and so promptly handed one over. I was then thanked for a good job done and off he went.

Taking it in turns, various family members did their bit to help backfill to a depth just above the casket, before leaving it for my colleague and I to finish. It was a lavish send-off which must have cost a small fortune. However, that was neither here nor there because, more importantly, it had been a husband's way of saying goodbye to the woman he sincerely loved, or - as he had put it himself - his queen. Oddly, after all the pomp and ceremony, the grave was never attended again.

CHAPTER 5

Halloween prank

Each year during leaf fall, a member of the street clean-
ing team would join us for a couple of days a week to
help tidy up. It was a mammoth task, which back then
(early 80's) meant meticulously raking each section by
hand on a fortnightly basis. It was a thankless task
throughout, but on a cold crisp morning it soon got the
circulation going. Time and again we'd be sent the same
chap. He was quite a character; always smiling and
happy to do anything. He undoubtedly brightened up
many a grey day, though I must say he was a few bricks
light of a load and extremely gullible.

On October 31st, 1983 (Halloween) I partially dug out a
new double-depth grave. The following morning fellow
worker Ted took our colleague to one side and said to
him, 'Today I have a very important job for you to do.
As yesterday was Halloween, we need to do a stock
check. I want you to walk around the cemetery and
check the graves to make sure that no zombies have
escaped.'. I smiled to myself, as Ted had tried that one on
me in my first year. Our colleague, however, simply froze
on the spot, his jaw dropped and his eyes widened. He

didn't cotton on, instead he replied, 'What? You want me to go on my own? What if the zombies get me?' Ted tried not to laugh and assured, 'They won't, it's daylight. You're quite safe now, be brave.' With that our colleague pulled on his coat, lit up a cigarette and off he went - much to our amusement. A short time later the mess-room door suddenly burst open and in fell our colleague. He was quite literally on his knees, ashen-faced, out of breath and blatantly panic-stricken. He shouted, 'Come quick! One's got away!'

I'm not sure who was the more surprised, him or us, as his hasty theatrical entrance made us all jump. With that Ted got up and said to him, 'Come with me.'. He walked across to a workbench and picked up a lump hammer and a pointed wooden stake, which he then handed to our colleague. 'You best show me where,' said Ted and off they both went. We had all guessed just where they were heading, but our curiosity meant that we just had to follow. Our workmate was not aware that I had been digging a grave, but nevertheless he should have known better. 'Over there!' he shouted, pointing in the direction of the freshly-dug grave. He then refused to go any closer, but Ted - now standing beside the grave - was having none of it. 'Come on! Come here, it's OK!' he said. Initially he took some persuading, but the man eventually plucked up the courage and, although extremely hesitant, did finally do as Ted asked. Ted then looked him in the face and said, 'Now, when I open these boards, you be ready. It must not escape, you must jump down and hammer the stake through the zombie's heart.' Our colleague said nothing but his face was a picture. 'On one,' said Ted. '3-2-1!' And, with that, Ted slid open the walk-boards but our frightened workmate dropped both the hammer and stake and was gone - not once did he look back. Of course, we all fell about laughing. 'I can't believe that anyone could fall for that,' said Ted as he lit up his pipe. When we finally caught up with our colleague, he was sitting in the mess. He must have chain-smoked a whole packet of cigarettes because the mess-room was filled with a thick, blue-grey haze. He jokingly made light of the incident, but when I asked him to help me finish digging the grave he point-blank refused, stating that he was putting in for a transfer.

Unfortunately our colleague was to fall foul of another of Ted's tricks when he sent him to the council stores with a written list of things to fetch. 'Hand this to the man and he will sort you out,' said Ted. The list read: one tube of elbow grease; one bubble for a spirit level; a handful of skyhooks; a sack of oil; and a glass hammer and rubber tacks. It was that easy!

CHAPTER 6

They're digging him up

The cemetery has always had what I deemed to be its regulars; those individuals who, no matter what the weather, would dutifully attend their loved one's grave. Many became familiar to me and over time I have befriended them and got to know them quite well. Some you could set your watch by, but none more so than one little old lady who would visit her son's grave no less than four times a day, every day. This ritual she continued to do up until her own death.

One morning my workmate and I began digging out the plot next to where this lady's son was buried. Engrossed in our work, neither my colleague nor I had seen this woman approaching. We only became aware of her presence when she abruptly yelled out loud, 'Oh my God! I can't believe it, they're digging him up! They're digging my son up!' Her startling outburst certainly got our attention and immediately we both looked across to where she was standing. Although she was situated some 20 yards from the dig, I guess at first glance it may well have appeared to look as if we were reopening her son's grave. Until now her family plot had been the last on the row and it may well have stayed that way if another family had not requested to purchase it.

Taking one step at a time, she gradually moved towards us until she came within a few feet of where we were working. She then pointed directly at us and screamed at the top of her voice: 'Grave robbers!' before falling to her knees in floods of tears. With both hands wrapped tightly around her head, she continued to cry out: 'They're digging him up! Why? Why?' To be frank, both my colleague and I were at a loss just what to do, but all the same we could not leave her in this state of mind. But as we both moved towards her, she quickly got up and marched off shouting, 'They're coming for me now! They're coming for me!' At this point I thought it best not to follow her, as it may have made the situation worse. Though by now she had made a swift exit.

A short time later, her husband arrived. He said, 'I'm sorry. My wife came home crying her heart out, saying that you were digging our son up. I told her not to be so daft, why would they be doing that? But she wouldn't have it, so she's sent me down to find out what's going on.' He could see quite clearly that all was in order and again apologised and explained that his wife had been beside herself following their son's unexpected death. He then asked when the funeral was and promised to keep his wife away until the burial was completed. However, within a couple of hours his wife was back sitting on a bench directly opposite to where we were working, though thankfully she was now less upset and a little more composed.

CHAPTER 7

You can't please everyone

On a typically cold February morning, I began digging out a 6ft reopen grave which had initially been dug at 7ft6. It was a Friday and, although the burial was not until the Monday, I had decided to get set up and started to make my life a little easier on the day. Come Monday I was met by a puzzled-looking undertaker, who told me that a member of the deceased's family had visited the grave and been shocked to discover that the gravedigger had opened the wrong plot. Somewhat concerned, I immediately rechecked my paperwork and the under-taker and myself cross-referenced the adjoining grave numbers, but all tallied - meaning it was correct. The grave had no headstone but, according to a family rela-tive, it should have been dug four plots further up the row. That assumption was incorrect, as the burial regis-ter showed that that plot had been pre-purchased and as yet remained unused. There was only one true way in which to confirm that the grave I had opened was correct and that was to simply check the nameplate on the coffin originally interred. So, with a fellow workmate and the undertaker as my witness, I dug down until I was stand-ing directly on top of the coffin below. This I call 'knocking on heaven's door' for if you gently tap the lid with your shovel, it does sound like you're knocking at a door. I was once asked 'what would you do if someone knocked back?' To be honest, you wouldn't see me for dust. Supported by nothing more than the lid of the hollow coffin below me, I crouched down and, equally spreading my weight to the outer edges, began to carefully scrape back soil to locate the nameplate. At this point you can't help but hope that the coffin lid holds, because if it doesn't and suddenly collapses, not only will the stench turn you green but you may find yourself knee-deep in human soup. This may sound far-fetched but, believe me, water does settle and collect in a coffin and, if disturbed, it can be highly unpleasant. After a few minutes I had located the nameplate, which I wiped clean with my glove before reading out the etched inscription. As expected, everything was in order and it was in fact the correct grave.

After the funeral had taken place and the mourners had all but dispersed, the undertaker - who purposely remained behind - told me that the same relative was still not convinced that it was the right grave. Not only that but they now believed I had dug the grave the wrong way round. Furthermore, they had stated that it had not been dug deep enough to allow room for a third interment. What a cheek!

This of course was not the case; they had said that the head of the coffin was not where the headstone would be. All Christian burials face east/west and in many parts of the cemetery, although the grave is correctly dug that way, the headstones are actually footstones - as was the case here. This is not uncommon; it's just the way the cemetery is set out. As for the correct depth, I can assure them that there remains ample space for a third burial. Finally, just to rub salt in my wounds, I was later to hear that this individual was planning to go to the newspapers and vowed to have both sets of remains exhumed. However, nothing ever came of it and I heard no more.

CHAPTER 8

The drunken gravedigger

Take it from me, gravedigging and beer do not mix! There's nothing worse than having a skinful the night before then having to go to work with a thumping hangover, knowing that you have to dig a grave. I have been there – it's horrible! Sleeping it off in a wheelbarrow is far from comfortable, and so is shovelling or bending coupled with a churning stomach, as this is guaranteed to bring it all up and make you violently ill.

I have seen colleagues standing in the bottom of a grave, hanging on to either the walk-boards or the shoring in a desperate attempt to stop the world from spinning. It's not pleasant. For one fellow colleague, however, it was a lesson he never did learn. After the death of his mother, our workmate inherited a small but comfortable amount of money. It was no secret that he was partial to a drink or three, but unfortunately the money, like the beer, went straight to his head and was quickly spent. His favourite pastime soon began to affect his work, and those around him became increasingly aware that his drunken antics were getting progressively worse. Most days he would disappear off site around mid-morning and not return until after three. He'd arrive at work drunk and go home drunk; he was quickly becoming a liability.

I recall one occasion when he had dug out a double-depth grave, which he duly dressed and made ready. No-one gave it a second thought, but when the funeral arrived all was not well. As the hearse left, the funeral director beckoned me and my workmate to come over to the grave. This we did and, on looking into the grave, we found the coffin to be wedged stuck, tilted on its side and resting a foot or so from the bottom. It was obvious that our drunken colleague had not entirely finished the dig, but had not informed anyone either. Instead he had just left it. Both the family and the undertaker were fuming and a formal complaint was lodged. Our colleague, however, somehow escaped any disciplinary proceedings much to the annoyance of us all. Beware, for your sins will eventually find you out – and, of course, they soon did.

One morning quite unexpectedly, our colleague's dear wife made a surprise visit to the cemetery. At the time a workmate and I were digging a grave close to where her unsuspecting husband was working. In a flash their eyes met and all hell broke loose as she began shouting and yelling at her other half. Clearly angered by whatever he had done, she progressed from the verbal onslaught to something more physical. We watched in utter disbelief as she removed her shoe and, with the heel of it, began battering him about the head. It was a frenzied no-holds bout which her half-cut husband could do little about. We were standing around 200 yards away, but could quite clearly hear the crack of leather against our colleague's head. The domestic continued as she proceeded to march him up the cemetery's main avenue. Her tactics, however, then changed as she replaced her shoe but continued to beat him first with a discarded plastic bottle then with a pretty hefty stick she had picked up. Intrigued and highly amused by what was unfolding before us, we both followed closely behind, bursting with laughter each time she scored a direct hit.

Like a naughty schoolboy, she then grabbed hold of his ear and physically dragged him into the superintendent's office. It was not long before they both simultaneously re-emerged and immediately went their separate ways. Our battered and bruised colleague said nothing of his past-ing and simply went back to work as though nothing had happened. Later that day our boss quietly told us what had been said. It appeared that he had squandered all the money and not paid the many outstanding bills. His wife had snapped, said she had had enough and threatened her husband with divorce. She had also demanded that the superintendent immediately sack him from his job. Once again though he was spared the latter, but the end was coming. His continued love of a lunchtime tipple was to prove too strong and, as a result, he was eventually dismissed. I never knew what became of him though I believe he did split from his wife before moving away, possibly to Blackpool.

The old timers often spoke of another colleague who liked nothing more than a lunchtime drink. I was told that his favourite place to hide and sleep it off was at the bottom of a grave. He was often found out-for-the-count, slumped at the bottom of his dig; he would even close the walk-boards above so he wouldn't be disturbed.

CHAPTER 9

One of the lads

Throughout the years I have worked at Newark Cemetery, I have seen many a boss come and go. None of them have stayed the course and, in my opinion, most have seemingly bluffed their way through a job which, in truth, they knew very little about. Apart from Mr Tate, I only ever welcomed one other. He was not a local man, but he was knowledgeable in all aspects of cemetery workings as he'd actually done the job. He had the experience and was a genuinely nice bloke, though in his heart I believe he would have much preferred to have remained just one of the lads. At the end of the day he had risen from a manual position to supervisor, climbing the next rung of the ladder but at times I think he found this extremely hard to swallow.

At the first opportunity he would close his office, put on his boots and - without any gripe - simply get stuck in with the rest of the lads. He would chat continually about his previous job. He would tell us his own gravedigging stories, of which there were many. He told how he'd single-handedly dug through stone and chalk and how he'd used small charges of dynamite to loosen it. No-one disbelieved him but we all pulled his leg, especially regarding the use of dynamite. At times he would get quite defensive and often rant and rave about how we didn't believe him, and that one day he would prove to us that he could dig a grave as well as the next man.

One Monday morning, as my colleague and I were emptying the rubbish bins, I suddenly noticed what appeared to be a freshly-backfilled grave. A closer inspection revealed that the grave had indeed been opened, though the question was: when? We were both puzzled by this and decided to inform our boss of our findings. He was not at all troubled by this, in fact he bore a somewhat smug grin as he proceeded to light up a rather large cigar. It was then that the penny finally dropped. He could not wait to tell my colleague and I that he and a co-worker of ours had dug the reopen grave on the Saturday; furthermore it had only taken them two-and-a-half hours to do so, with an additional hour to backfill. Self-praise indeed! He went on to brag, 'See, I told you all that I could do it. I've still got the knack.' I didn't know quite what to say, though in all honesty none of us could believe that our boss had actually kept details of the burial so secret. Apparently no-one had been more surprised than the colleague who had been conned into helping him. He had volunteered to work the Saturday, believing his time would be spent putting up the town's Christmas decorations, only to find himself rush-digging a grave for midday. Alas, walls have ears and news that the superintendent himself had dug a grave reached far and wide. He was reprimanded for his actions and forbidden to do it again. But it didn't bother him in the slightest, because he had proved that he too was a gravedigger and still just one of the lads. Sadly he left in 1990; he was the last official cemetery superintendent.

CHAPTER 10

Floral tributes

After backfilling a grave, the final task is to place all the flowers, bouquets and wreaths. It's not rocket science, though there is a certain way in which it's done. Presenting them in the correct family order is important, as this highlights the final display. To do this means you have to read each individual card so you can sort them into priority. Immediate family are put on first, with the tribute from the husband, wife or partner being placed at the head of the arrangement. Brothers, sisters, nieces, uncles and aunties are then laid down the centre of the grave. All other tributes are sited in neat rows running parallel on either side. Bouquets are placed last, usually at the foot of the dig, though if there are many they are positioned around the edge of the burial to give a neat all-round finish. I take great pride in presenting a well-ordered floral display, although getting the balance right can be a challenge. The finishing touches are the most important and I have often been thanked for the way in which it has been done. A good display can look fantastic, though I personally find that 'less is best' as too many wreaths can look cluttered. I find that three evenly-spaced rows are perfect. Five family wreaths down the centre and one each side of the shoulder, presented in the form of a cross, also makes for a good display.

In this day and age it's hard to believe, but occasionally there are funerals which no-one attends. I have witnessed a number of burials where the turnout has been just the vicar, a funeral director and his four pallbearers. At one such funeral, a bearer placed a single carnation by the grave. He told me that he'd found it in the back of the hearse and, rather than throw it away, he'd asked if it could be placed on the grave. It was a nice gesture!

On the other hand, I have seen some big funerals with lots of wreaths. Burials of the travelling community are classic affairs, boasting some of the grandest displays you will ever see. They are imaginative and quite unique! To date the most impressive tribute I have seen was a 4ft tall horse and gypsy caravan, made entirely out of carnations. It must have taken hours to complete as it was a detailed work of art and must have cost a small fortune. Other bizarre tributes include chairs, teapots, dartboards, whisky bottles, horseshoes, windmills, tankards, baskets of fruit; the list is endless. Without doubt the most unusual wreath I have seen stood 3ft tall and was designed in the shape of a well-known bottle of face cream. Placing these often takes longer than it does to backfill the grave. As a rule it's a three-man job, as they can be quite heavy but also fragile, and so can be easily damaged. It's a task that cannot be rushed but, once complete, you just have to stand back and admire the many colours, shapes and designs. It is a sight to be seen.

After one such funeral I recall that an old woman approached me and asked quite politely, 'Please will you read me all the cards, as I cannot read.' Being new to the job I was unaware that she was known to my older colleagues, who had in fact pointed her in my direction. Ignoring their cheeky grins, I agreed and in the process spent nearly two hours reading her all the cards on well over 100 wreaths. It took so long that my workmates had actually packed up and gone home. I wasn't to fall for that again!

No two funerals of the travelling community are ever the same. Possibly the most joyful send-off I've seen saw the undertaker briskly walking ahead of a five-piece band, who were merrily playing a lively blend of Irish folk-cum-New Orleans jazz. Behind this came a black and white horse pulling a flat, open-backed cart bearing the coffin. The family followed closely behind and at the rear was a similar-looking horse pulling a second cart laden with wreaths. The funeral had a nostalgic 1960's rag and bone feel about it. It was extremely authentic with classic old-style vans and cars which were a real head-turner. It could easily have been a scene straight from an episode of *Heartbeat*.

When it comes to handling flowers, some of my colleagues have not only had hay fever where their eyes have streamed continuously, but some have also suffered allergies and developed itchy red blotches and nasty rashes when certain types of flowers have irritated their skin. For one young lad this was more like a curse. He had only to be near a flower and he'd begin sneezing uncontrollably, his face would turn red and, within minutes, his cheeks and eyes would puff up to twice their size. It was frightening to see and the only way he could stop it was to immerse his entire head in cold water. I did once work with a man who refused point-blank to handle flowers or wreaths in any way whatsoever. He was a moody old so-and-so and when I asked him why, he simply replied, 'I don't do flowers. It's a woman's job!'

CHAPTER 11

The unknown priest

While workmen were demolishing and clearing a site for reuse, they discovered under a stone floor the remains of a crypt which contained a lead-lined coffin. Although it was known that a burial ground with a hospital or church had once occupied the site, it was believed that nothing now remained. It was an unexpected discovery that quite literally brought the job to a complete stand-still. It was a mystery!

At the time I recall being told that the coffin had been opened and that archaeologists had concluded the remains may have been of a priest, who had been buried under the floor of the church sometime in the 13th or 14th century. I can't now bring to mind where exactly in Newark the remains were discovered. It may have been around the Mill Gate area of the town, but it's the St Leonard's Hospital, which stood on the north side of North Gate at the south end of the Lincoln Road viaduct, which seems to ring a bell. A stone building is known to have stood here and 170 burials were found dating back to the 13th century, which indicates that this may have been the place. The re-interment of the unknown priest took place at Newark Cemetery. I did not dig the grave but was present on the day of the reburial. The lead-lined coffin had been placed inside a hefty wooden crate which only just fitted into the back of a large van. It was heavy - extremely heavy - and although my boss, the van driver, three fellow colleagues and a man from the environmental department and I all helped to lift it, we struggled to manhandle it to get it graveside. There was no minute's silence nor were any prayers said and, once the crate was lowered, the grave was simply sprinkled with quicklime and then backfilled and left unmarked and forgotten forever. To this day, the name of the priest still remains a complete mystery!

CHAPTER 12

Personal achievement

The 17th of November, 1992 was a typical autumn day; it was overcast, grey and drizzly, but neither windy nor cold. It was perfect conditions for a bit of gravedigging. I was nearing 30 years of age, still young and, if I say so myself, in my prime and at the peak of fitness when I took it on myself to dig and fully complete four reopen graves in one solitary seven-and-three-quarter hour shift. All four were in Newark Cemetery. There was no actual reason for me to even attempt this but I just had to know if I could do it. My colleagues thought I was mad and of course there's always one that lays down the gauntlet by announcing that it can't be done. It was a personal challenge and a test of my own ability and, yes, it was a tall order but the opportunity was there and I was at least going to give it a go. With hindsight, it seems a bit daft now.

My working day did not begin until 7.30am and daylight was slow in coming. In fairness, for the first dig a colleague did cast-back spoil for me, but he soon decided that one dig was enough for anyone and so he simply left me to it. By lunch I had fully completed two digs and had started a third, and by close of play I had completely finished them all. Each dig was regulation depth (4ft6) and of similar consistency, which meant they were moderately straightforward to dig. In my favour, none of the graves were shored (optional, back then) which undoubtedly made it possible for me to achieve my goal. Take nothing away; it was no easy feat, as there was a lot of spoil to shift in a relatively small amount of time. Although it had all been unnecessary, I was genuinely pleased with my accomplishment, though it was undoubtedly a one-off and something I would never intentionally attempt again.

Sixteen years later, now a little older and a lot less agile, I was to suddenly receive a draft proposal for the action in the event of a flu pandemic. Throughout the UK, all local authorities had been asked to put together a disaster plan in case of an outbreak. I was asked how many graves I could dig in a week. In truth, the whole idea that an outbreak was becoming more likely was not only alarming but had been far from my thoughts, in fact it had never once crossed my mind. With an immediate answer being sought, I was actually stumped and unsure of just what to say. How long is a piece of string? I had never contemplated this situation and so was not prepared to give an immediate answer. At the height of a pandemic, it was predicted that in a worst-case scenario Newark Cemetery itself could potentially see full burial interments rise from two per week to 35, while cremated remains could total 28, resulting in there being 63 interments in a seven-day period. It was only later when I sat down and thought about it in greater detail that I realised it would be a near impossible workload to complete. In addition, it was all well and good committing me to one place, but the sheer volume of work would in theory also include the other 107 churchyards and cemeteries I now visit. I can call on a few people to lend a hand, but they might not want to, or they themselves might be caring for sick family relatives. It did not bear thinking about! Until it happens - if it happens - I have put it to the back of my mind. I do not dwell on it, or else I'd never sleep at night. For the time being it is best forgotten and, better still, let's hope it never happens.

CHAPTER 13

Buried together

Life is life and so, tragically, from time to time accidents do occur. Thankfully, however, it's extremely uncommon for me to be asked to bury two family relatives on the same day. The deceased, depending on how closely they are related, may be interred together in one double-depth grave, or they may be laid to rest side-by-side in two single-depth graves. Whichever is chosen, double funerals such as these are quite unusual, though the procedure differs little from a conventional burial. It is actually quite eerie to stand and watch two hearses pull up at a graveside. A colleague once said to me, 'It's unnerving. I've seen many funerals, but seeing two coffins being laid to rest at the same time has, for whatever reason, given me goosebumps. I've come over all cold.'

I will not forget my first double funeral. It was of two unrelated persons who had been killed in a road traffic accident, and they were to be buried side-by-side. I recall that on the morning of the funeral, the thin dividing wall which marginally separated the two graves had collapsed. This left a huge square hole measuring 7ft by 7ft. What I remember most is that during the interment four of the eight bearers lowering the coffin had to precariously stand back-to-back on two centre walk-boards, which at best measured 20 inches wide. Basically, this left four men and two coffins balanced in mid-air with just the woods to support them. The funeral director, quite wisely, made it clear that he was not happy for his pallbearers to do this and would have preferred to have interred the coffins separately, one at a time. The family, however, were adamant that as the deceased were close friends and had died together, then they must be interred together at the same time.

Thankfully the pallbearers were not only light on their feet but were able to safely co-ordinate their lowering procedure with complete professionalism, so preventing any untimely mishaps from occurring. At another such funeral I was asked to be present, as the family had requested that after the first coffin had been interred in what was a double-depth grave, they wished for me to backfill to six inches above the coffin. This meant me having to partially undress the grave, backfill in front of all those watching, then enter the grave to carefully level it out before re-dressing and discreetly retreating to the sidelines. The second interment then took place. Even now, after many years in the job, I still find this procedure uncomfortable to complete in front of ever-watchful eyes.

I've always found it worthy of note how death seemingly comes to call. For instance, in January 1994 over an 11-day period I dug out three adjoining, double-depth graves for the same family and, believe it or not, years later two of the graves were reopened within a few months of each other. I can go months without an infant burial and then I'll get one, and within a fortnight I can almost guarantee there will be another; this is seemingly the same with Roman Catholic burials! Out in the villages it can be two years since I last visited a churchyard, only to return for a second burial within a week of the first and then not return again for a further two years. It's amazing how burials also seem to come in clusters, where three or four burials will take place in neighbouring parishes in relatively quick succession, and often I have been able to predict with accuracy which village I will visit next. I must say that I actually find this a bit creepy! I did find reference to a graveyard superstition that actually fits nicely with the above. 'One funeral makes three' - if there has been a long time without a death in a community it means that when the next person dies, two more will die in quick succession.

CHAPTER 14

The trouble with ashes is...

You would think that digging a hole for an interment of ashes, which is no different to digging a posthole, would be a straightforward task. Not so! The digging of ash plots was usually left to my older colleagues but for one old timer, whom I'll call Mr Forgetful, there was always a hitch.

January 2nd, 9.30am, first day back after Christmas and New Year, and my colleague dropped a right clanger. Asked by the foreman he proceeded to dig out the hole, but when the undertaker arrived to inter the ashes, both he and the family found that no hole had been dug. The foreman was called and, in front of everyone, he was left with the uncomfortable task of both digging the plot as well as having to apologise to both parties. This left the foreman not only embarrassed but angry, very angry. But to some extent he was also somewhat puzzled, as he had seen our colleague preparing to dig it. A bitter row erupted between the two and the end result was that Mr. Forgetful had simply misread the paperwork. Instead of digging plot number 420, he had dug 402. He had located the correct row but had not double-checked the reference number and so, as a result, he was some 18 plots adrift. It was an easy mistake to make but our colleague offered no apology, blamed his overindulgence at the New Year's festivities and simply walked out on sick leave.

Not remembering to backfill an ash plot was another of our colleague's favourite tricks. One in particular remained open for two days and, if it hadn't have been for a vigilant funeral director, would most certainly have remained open for a lot longer. For the family to have returned and found it still open would have been bad enough, but if anyone had removed or taken the casket then it would undoubtedly have been front page news.

Finding any plot within the cemetery's Garden of Remembrance was never easy, as the plan was extremely hard to follow. As foreman I handed my trusted colleague the paperwork for a burial of ashes and he assured me he knew exactly where he was digging, so I left him to it. After the interment I returned to make sure he'd backfilled it, only to discover that he had actually dug the wrong one. It was two rows out! Like all staff he was aware that this section had no row 'I' or row 'O', yet on locating the plot he had foolishly included them, hence the mistake. It could not be left like this so I reported my findings, only to be bluntly told to put it right or heads would roll. So, while my colleague carefully reopened the plot he'd dug, I dug out the correct one and then swiftly - so no-one would see - the casket was removed and duly placed in its correct position and all was well.

I once asked a fellow workmate to dig out a new double-depth plot; bearing in mind that an average-sized casket measures approximately 13 × 9 inches, therefore you dig to a bare minimum of 15 × 11. He was quick to complete the job but, on checking his handiwork, I found that the hole only measured 11 × 9, and was barely half the depth it should have been. He was not best pleased that I had picked up on this and even less pleased when I asked if he'd correct it. On looking into the hole, he stated that a good funeral director could easily get a casket in there... I'm not sure how! Digging the hole too small so the casket does not fit has, to my knowledge, happened just the once. I recall the superintendent at the time having to apologise to the bereaved family before leaving them graveside while he frantically searched the cemetery to find someone to come and re-dig it. Thankfully on that occasion I was spared this embarrassing task, though the digger himself never lived it down.

Exhuming a casket of ashes has its own problems, for locating their exact whereabouts in an 8ft × 4ft family plot can become a game of hide-and-seek. They could have been interred anywhere within that space. Usually the first interment would be placed at the head, but if there have been multiple burials then the job becomes more complicated and you could end up digging any number of holes. More often than not, ashes are buried within the Garden of Remembrance and so exhuming them is a somewhat easier procedure. However, as with all caskets, great care must be taken because the wooden box may simply fall apart in your hands. Once the casket has been found, then it's down on your knees with a trowel as you begin to carefully search for a nameplate. When identification is complete you can then begin to lift it, usually piece by piece. The main objective is not to pierce or split the polythene bag in which the ashes are contained, for if you do then you will need a brush and dustpan.

With good reason, the spreading or scattering of ashes is not encouraged in Newark Cemetery. I do recall a time while I was mowing the grass that I did not see the scattered remains and I ran my machine through and over them. As a result the ash stuck to both my wet boots and to the tyres on my machine, thereby spreading them much further afield than originally intended. As daft as it may seem, I once fully dug out a six-foot double-depth grave and at the bottom I dug a 16×12 inch hole. In it was interred a casket of ashes; although there remains enough room for two full interments, it seemed a bizarre thing to do and it's certainly the deepest burial of ashes I have done.

CHAPTER 15

Did I not tell you
it was a casket?

On the 26th May 1997 I was promoted to cemetery foreman. Among the many tasks I had to oversee, it was my job to make sure that graves were dug on time and in the right place. They must be of regulation depth, adequately shored and, more importantly, the dimensions of each dig must be accurate to allow the coffin to be interred without a hitch. Unfortunately, no matter how well you prepare yourself, if the wrong information is supplied then things can go horribly wrong.

The ultimate gravedigging nightmare is when the coffin does not fit the grave! You fear for that day, more so as foreman, because you are held personally responsible. And in the summer of 2001 that dreaded day came. I had not dug the grave, but nevertheless found it more than embarrassing. The only consolation was that it was neither the fault of my colleagues or indeed myself. However, both the family and funeral director were not to know this, and it was me they saw so me they blamed. I was also expected to put things right.

The grave was traditional in shape though the dig was bigger than normal, as the actual coffin size was 6ft7 × 28 inches with standard fixed handles. On completion the grave was duly dressed and made ready for their arrival. It was nearing the end of my lunch break when the hearse and cortege arrived, so I hadn't seen them pass by. But as I and my colleagues were preparing to follow them up, I suddenly received a phone call. A stuttering voice on the other end then proceeded to announce that there was a problem graveside and the coffin could not be interred. I was asked, 'Did I not tell you it was a casket and not a traditional-shaped coffin?' 'Pardon?' I replied, not quite believing what I'd just heard. 'No, you did not,' I added, but before I could say anything more, they hung up. With that bombshell dropped, my colleagues and I somewhat worriedly made our way to the grave. On our arrival we were met with a deathly silence. This, coupled with the mourners' scornful stares, was extremely unnerving; it was awful. The casket had been placed by the grave, resting solely on two trestle legs while the immediate family looked on from afar. I tried to explain to both parties what had occurred, but neither was interested. As far as they were concerned, it was my fault. And furthermore, what was I going to do about it? Well, you can't fit an oblong casket into a traditionally-shaped hole, so it was a simple case of roll up our sleeves, undress the grave, remove the shoring, re-shape, re-size and re-dig it.

To complete the above put me in total breach of Health and Safety rules, and in effect I was putting my own job on the line. Following H&S and council guidelines would have meant me having to backfill the grave to just below the shoring. This would then have to be removed and the grave reshaped before shoring was replaced. The grave would then have to be re-dug to the required depth. But to do that would have taken about an hour! This was time I didn't have, as a second funeral would soon be upon us, so I decided that the commonsense approach was best and, with no time to lose, I cracked on with the task in hand. If I hadn't, then the two funerals would have crossed and the situation would have been even worse. Thankfully my decision paid off and within half an hour the committal was complete and the mourners had dispersed. The icy cold stares we received were enough to turn us all to stone, as everyone was blaming the gravediggers. The family concerned did receive a letter of apology, which explained that we were not at fault and that a simple administrative error had occurred. I, on the other hand, did not receive a letter of apology. I was told in no uncertain terms that I had disregarded Health and Safety regulations and, in the process, had put my colleagues, pallbearers and members of the public at risk. I was to be thankful that I was being allowed to keep my job - and for this I should be grateful. I was fuming!

The incident was all set to become front page news, but somehow it was craftily averted. Personally, as this was found to have been an internal administration error, I believe it was overlooked. If blame could have been pinned at the feet of the gravedigger, then I'm quite sure that I would most certainly have been sacked.

CHAPTER 16

New challenge

In January 2003 I left my municipal position at Newark Town Council and started my own gravedigging business. It was something that I'd always considered doing and the timing could have not been better. It was an opportunity not to be missed and, although it was a big leap, I was in no doubt that it was the right move.

I had worked for NTC for over 20 years. I had enjoyed the time immensely but was now looking forward to being my own boss, going it alone and seeking out the different challenges that certainly lay ahead. In fairness, I wasn't completely saying goodbye to Newark Cemetery as I had picked up the contract to dig the graves there.

Within a month I returned to digging graves in the many villages that surround Newark, although this was to quickly extend into Lincolnshire and occasionally beyond. The last village dig I had done was back in 2001, which had been at the request of a friend. Before that I had not dug outside Newark Cemetery gates for nearly 20 years. It was a welcome return as I never expected the opportunity to come around again. I'm glad it did, as from week to week I can now find myself in any one of the 107 different cemeteries/churchyards I now visit.

I prefer digging a grave in a quiet village churchyard than digging at Newark Cemetery, though this is simply because I'm so used to working there. The sheer variety of places I now visit is vast and with each new place comes a fresh challenge, as I have no idea of what I may be up against. Most village churchyards are idyllic, peaceful places; an early summer's morning or a late evening is by far my favourite time for working. A summer's eve, the smell of freshly-mown grass, birds singing and church bells ringing... you can't beat it. However, I do draw the line at the smell of a barbeque wafting close to where you're working, as after a hard day's graft it's far from fair. In many ways I'm quite fortunate, as I would consider the area in which I now work to be reasonably good digging. Don't get me wrong, very few graves dig out like Skegness beach and, believe me, I've slogged hard over many a difficult dig. I have spent many an hour toiling late into the evening only to return at daybreak to finish up. At times I have been pushed up to and beyond my limit, but at the end of the day a deadline is a deadline and this is something I've never failed to meet.

There was, however, one occasion when a dig came within a whisker's width of getting the better of me and it was at Long Bennington during the summer of 2006. It was a blisteringly hot day with no breeze and no shade. From start to finish I struggled to break through the dry, clay earth and, although I had help from my old mate, Jack Hammer, progress was tediously slow. I had run out of water and my shoulders and neck were red raw from the heat of the sun. To make things worse, I had a belter of a headache.

If truth be told, I could endure no more and was literally on the brink of conceding when, from nowhere, a local villager kindly brought me a cold glass of water. It was without doubt the best drink I'd ever had in my life. Then came a morale boost that definitely saved the day when, within minutes of each other, my wife brought both food and a thirst-quenching drink and my brother (digging colleague) arrived with a cooling ice cream. After taking time out I began to feel human again and, as I wasn't going to let the job beat me, I continued with my tough task even though I did not finish until 9.30pm. Although this had been just a single-depth grave, it had taken me nearly nine hours to complete. I had never spent this much time on a 4ft6 dig, though graves at Coddington and Flawborough have come pretty close.

CHAPTER 17

Wrong grave

Well, I guess that at some point it happens to the best of us, but I had only been self-employed for just six months when I came close to making the biggest cock-up of my career. I had dug and completed a reopen grave, only to realise that I had actually reopened the wrong one. I had not only dug it, but had dressed it in readiness for the interment. Subconsciously, while completing the task, I had had this nagging feeling that something was wrong but had failed to pick up on it. I should have known better and double-checked beforehand, but at the time other matters preoccupied my mind. At midday I left site, but at home - and only by sheer chance - I had decided to catch up with paperwork in the spare time I had. It was then when I checked back that I suddenly realised the grave I had dug did not match with the instructions issued. I can't put into words how I actually felt at that precise moment in time. It was 1pm and the panic button had well and truly been pressed. After self-rollicking myself, I phoned my colleague and by 1.15pm I was back on-site confirming my worst fear. I should have reopened the neighbouring grave, the one which the spoil heap was now covering. Honestly, what an idiot! I could have sacked myself!

I quickly threw aside the green matting and my colleague and I swiftly backfilled the grave. By the time we had finished and put everything right, there was just over an hour left in which to re-dig the correct plot. The adrenalin pumped and my heart pounded as I got well and truly stuck in. The clock was ticking and the pressure was immense, but I remained positive that I would complete within the time, unless of course they were untraditionally early.

Fortunately it was not an over-demanding dig and, by pushing myself that extra bit, I was able to finish with just minutes to spare. Expecting their imminent arrival, the grave was quickly dressed before we both retreated to the cool shade of the trees. There we waited, and waited. If I'd have known that the cortege was going to roll up some 18 minutes late, then I would not have driven myself so hard. On the other hand I had prevented what could have been a costly own goal.

Thankfully no-one but my colleague and I were any the wiser and, although I was really annoyed with myself, I was grateful that I'd spotted it in time to be able to deal with it accordingly. This had been a close shave, a wake-up call and a swift reminder not to be complacent and so forget rule one: always check your paperwork and the plot numbers before you start digging, or you might just be caught out.

CHAPTER 18

A funeral on a Sunday

It had been estimated that up to 2000 people would be attending this high-profile funeral. On police advice, it was approved that this interment should take place on a Sunday because it would be quieter and thereby cause less disruption around Newark's town centre. How times have changed; in days gone by a burial on the Sabbath would have been frowned upon, and if the old timers knew they'd surely be turning in their graves.

The interment was of a young man who had been murdered. When arranging the burial, the family had been told that, although they had pre-purchased a plot beside other family graves, there was now not enough space in which to bury their loved one. Understandably, they were not best pleased though the reason hadn't been fully explained to them. Consequently they were told to go and speak to the gravedigger as the final decision would be his. In truth this was not the case, but unfortunately I was caught in the middle and left to sort it out. Although the family fully understood my concerns regarding possible collapse and the lack of available space, they would not change their minds. It was made quite clear to me that they had purchased this particular plot and were insistent that, one way or another, it would be used, even if they had to dig the grave themselves.

For a traditional burial there would not have been a problem, but when interring a large American-style casket then the lack of space between surrounding graves becomes a major concern. It was a tight squeeze as this double-depth dig measured 8ft long by 39 inches wide. As a precaution I had taken extra measures and had fully shored the dig from top to bottom, though I was still sceptical as to whether it would actually stand. A collapse at any time is disastrous but, as this was going to be such a big funeral, I did not want any mishaps. The family had requested that all spoil be removed from sight, which for once I was glad to do as it relieved pressure and additional weight from the immediate area.

At 2.30pm on the day of the funeral, the grave was made ready and all was fine. I, however, was feeling really anxious which wasn't helped when the undertaker suddenly called and announced that he was nearing the cemetery and could I lay out a third lowering strap. The mourners were arriving in their droves and there was I frantically searching for a matching strap, which of course was not in its usual place. Fortunately, in the nick of time I found one before hastily retreating from view. As far as the eye could see, walking five abreast, the mourners arrived. It was a remarkable sight but as they neared the grave they all broke ranks and made a hasty beeline towards the grave. It was like a battle charge, as they seemingly jostled for the best graveside position. I had never seen anything like it.

Two striking white horses with crowns of black feathers pulled a white carriage, which contained the gunmetal coloured casket. Three grey limousines and a convoy of five lorries, laden with floral tributes, slowly followed behind. Eight family members carried the casket which they duly lowered into the grave. Happily there were no last-minute hiccups and, once the undertaker stood clear, I could finally breathe a huge sigh of relief.

I had been prepared for a lengthy backfill but dusk fell and darkness came too quickly, thus beating me to it. Site-lights and the headlights from two vehicles were all that lit the way as the job seemingly dragged on and on. I had never seen so many floral displays, in fact it took three of us over an hour to place and present them in the correct order. The job was finally completed at 7pm. It had been a long, tiring and - to some extent - quite a stressful day, but all was now done and I could once again sleep easy.

CHAPTER 19

Woodland burial

Hill Holt Wood can be found approximately eight miles out of Newark. It is a private wood, a secluded, hidden, green space sited close to the A46 bypass heading towards Lincoln. Many pass it each day without actually knowing it's there. It was here in 2005 that I was to dig my first green/woodland grave. The actual procedure is no different to digging any other grave, but what was unique was the unusual and unfamiliar location. Far from the madding crowd, deep in the woods and concealed from view, what an idyllic place to be laid to rest. Alas, for me personally, what spoilt this beautiful setting was the constant hum of the busy by-pass.

I had been told that my dig was only the ninth to have taken place there and that it would possibly be the last. The whole idea of this type of burial is for the grave to be left unmarked and, with time, become overgrown and so become part of the natural surroundings. Unfortunately, although the public in principle agreed to the owner's request, both markers and wreaths had been placed on graves. Bulbs had also been planted which were not native to the wood and, as a result, a decision had been made to not allow any further burials.

The dig I was to do was to be found in a small clearing, encircled on all sides by young, maturing trees. The sun streamed through the canopy and while at ground level I was sheltered by dense undergrowth, above me and the tree line blew a stormy, spring gale. Though I welcomed it, I was surprised by how well the surrounding trees protected the area below. The only real drawback was the long hike in bringing in equipment as there was no easy access. The whole area was noticeably boggy and wet underfoot, which did not entirely bode well. Nevertheless, despite the many roots that criss-crossed the area, the sticky clay dig proved easy to remove and, more importantly, I did not hit water until I was just over 4ft.

It was great to be able to take time out and sit on the walk-boards, dangling my legs over the edge while eating my snap and drinking a hot brew. Around me there was a wealth of wildlife, including a very noisy woodpecker which was seemingly knocking holes into every tree. Even the elusive cuckoo made a brief appearance. I had a very pleasant morning to say the least.

The coffin was made entirely of wicker and the body wrapped in what looked like muslin cloth. I must admit this type of burial certainly appealed to me so much that it started me thinking. Maybe I should look for a small plot of land which I could develop into a green woodland burial site. For two years I rolled this idea around my head. I spoke with undertakers, checked out other burial sites and duly researched the whole idea in full.

I concluded that it was possible and in May 2007 I found a five-acre piece of land with potential. It had good access, no near neighbours, did not flood, and indeed ticked all the right boxes. Financially it was possible and environmentally it was suitable, and I decided to proceed. I was buzzing with both enthusiasm and ideas but my hopes were cruelly dashed when I was gazumped at the last minute. It was a blow, but I didn't dwell on it. To this day I still quietly keep both eyes and ears open on the off-chance that I spot another potential piece of land.

There is no law that states that you cannot be buried in your own back garden. However, for various reasons it is not encouraged. I did once dig a double-depth grave in a paddock close to the deceased's family farm. It was a working farm and was a hive of activity, so it did feel strange and intrusive working so close to the family cottage. To openly chat with relatives in a laid-back manner seemed odd, though they in turn were moderately intrigued by how a grave was dug. It was certainly a one-off experience which I'm pleased to have been a part of, but I can only imagine the technical difficulties you would face if everyone was buried at home. This I can never see happening, although cemeteries and churchyards across the country are filling up and, with no vacant land available, it could in theory become a more frequent request.

CHAPTER 20

Spooky churchyard

Of all the churchyards that I now regularly visit, I would declare East Stoke to be one of the creepiest. This somewhat remote yet neatly-kept graveyard has a rather odd feel about it – it's as if you're being watched! For the most part this may be down to the tall, lifelike figure of an angel which rises high above all the other headstones. This dominant figure, with its chilling fixed gaze, is enough to raise the hairs on the back of your neck. Although it is just a monument to the dead, it is unsettling to say the least, and when working there your eyes seem to be constantly drawn towards it. It's quite eerie and I have often said to my colleagues that if I happen to look up and the head of the statuette has turned around to be watching me, then I'm out of there. I have heard talk that the figurine is said to weep real tears, but as yet I haven't seen any.

I once dug a grave there that turned out to be rather intriguing. The gravedigger who had originally dug it some ten years previously, had forewarned me that he had unearthed a large number of bones. Most had been broken fragments, although there had also been many complete skulls. These, along with any larger bones, he had placed in bags and they had been reburied back in the grave after the committal. On reopening the grave, I immediately started to find small shards of bone. The deeper I got the more I unearthed; the amount was unbelievable. In order for me to get a reasonable depth, I firstly had to remove some of the bags that the previous gravedigger had reburied. Although he'd bagged up many of the bigger bones, the spoil heap was littered with the remnants of smaller pieces. It was quite worrying as each shovelful continued to unearth yet more and more bone, but the question remained why was it all here? After the funeral I spoke to the vicar, but he too could shed no light on just why there were so many human remains in one solitary place. However, there were a few possible explanations.

In 1646 the plague raged through the village of East Stoke and in that year alone the burial register has entries for 161 burials, stating that seven score and nineteen (159) died of the plague. If a plague pit had been dug, then the back of the church would have been the ideal position. To mark the whereabouts of such a pit, a carved engraving was usually made on the stonework indicating where the pit was, but I could find no such mark.

In 1487 the battle of East Stoke Field was fought near to where the church stands. 7,000 men were said to have died that day and their bodies littered the surrounding fields. It is possible that some of the dead may have been buried in mass graves within the churchyard.

The final explanation - and the most likely - is that at some point in time the church had been extended. In order to lay the foundations, workmen would have had to clear and remove part of the burial ground. Any remains that were disturbed would have been reburied near to where they were originally found.

Whatever the true reason, East Stoke churchyard is a spooky place. I have dug many a grave on a dark winter's evening, but I can honestly say that I would not feel comfortable digging here, no way, especially alone!

CHAPTER 21

Opening a vault

I had agreed to meet with a stonemason to discuss the intended procedure for opening up a burial vault. I had originally dug the grave some 18 years previously, but I could not recall how it had been constructed. I was aware that it had been a double vault, but could not bring to mind if the chamber walls had been constructed either single or double brick in thickness. What the stonemasons were keen to know was how the remaining compartment had been sealed. Had it been concreted and reinforced, or had it simply been sealed with paving slabs?

Once the headstone and surrounding kerb set had been removed, I began digging to locate the top of the vault. This I quickly found and, once all the spoil had been removed, it was evident that it had been sealed using 3in paving slabs and that the surrounding vault walls were just one brick thick. I stood back and watched with astonishment as the stonemason, somewhat precariously I might add, simply stood on top of the vault and began hammering an iron bar between the cemented joints. He was convinced that the inside would be knee-deep in smelly, stagnant water. I remember thinking to myself that if it was full of water and those slabs suddenly gave way, then he'd be in for one hell of a unpleasant surprise. Luckily for him they held his weight and in no time at all they were removed, revealing the vacant chamber below. The floor beneath had been concreted but, more importantly, the vault was both dry and clean. The inside dimensions were not as big as I had expected, as it only measured 7ft × 3ft × 4ft3 in depth. Ample you may think, but at the time of opening I hadn't been issued with the actual coffin size. Usually for this type of burial, an oak or an American-styled casket is used, and they are wider and bulkier than a traditional coffin. I mentioned this to the stonemason who was not at all happy with the prospect of having to possibly widen and lengthen the vault. To put minds at rest, a call was made to the undertaker and, thankfully, it revealed that although the coffin was of solid oak it was traditional in shape, with casket handles. In comparison to the size of the vault it was small and so would be a neat fit.

Oddly the family had requested that once the coffin had been interred, the chamber must be backfilled to a depth of 18ins with sharp sand. Apparently the deceased had a phobia about being buried in the wet and had left instructions that his coffin be packed in sand. My maths was somewhat rusty, but my digging colleague quickly worked out that the volume needed was approximately one ton and he was spot-on. After the sand was placed, the stonemason laid a piece of 1in plyboard, covered by reinforcing mesh, on which concrete was poured. Once it was levelled out, the slabs were re-fixed and the grave was finally topped up with spoil.

CHAPTER 22

Unpleasant task

One of the drawbacks of being a gravedigger is that at some point in time you may be called upon to exhume a body. Thankfully it's not an everyday occurrence but nevertheless, if an undertaker even utters the word 'exhumation', your mind begins racing as you immediately begin to visualise what lies ahead. So far I have only done one full exhumation. Without doubt the task was unpleasant, but I was fortunate as my first job was pretty straightforward. I had been lucky enough to have worked in good draining land, which made life somewhat easier. Fellow colleagues have told me about removals they have done when working in heavy, sticky clay on waterlogged land. I have heard stories of gravediggers wading chin-deep in nasty, foul-smelling water to exhume a body. Even I would think twice about working in those conditions as it would be extremely unpleasant, but at the end of the day it's all part of the job.

The exhumation process can often be a costly and lengthy procedure and there is no real guarantee that the Home Office will grant permission and issue a licence. On this occasion, however, the family had a valid reason for exhuming the body of their child and so permission was granted and a date was set.

I can fully understand the Health and Safety aspect of this type of task, but surely commonsense prevails. For this job alone I had to go that extra mile and, in order to follow HSE guidelines, I had to provide disposable coveralls, goggles and masks, disposable gloves, wellingtons, quicklime, disinfectant, a generator, lights and screening. Wearing the appropriate clothing restricts all movement and, at over 6ft in depth, it is uncomfortable to say the least. However, with two Environmental Health officers present, it was in my best interests to look both professional and competent at what I was doing.

At 5am I had begun to uncover the child's coffin; at this point I swapped shovel for trowel and carefully began removing spoil from around the outer edge and under one end. At this point you must not be too heavy-handed as you want the coffin to remain intact. Conditions were dry, thus helping preserve the coffin, allowing me to lift one end just enough to feed a thick piece of polythene along the underside. A set of webbings were then placed underneath and slowly, inch by inch, four men lifted it out while I precariously supported the underside. The coffin was then placed by the undertaker into another coffin, before being removed from site. Quicklime was thrown in and around the grave, before being simply backfilled and reinstated to the highest degree. It had been a trouble-free task and I was satisfied with how well it had gone. By 6.20am the job was declared finished. Although exhumations are out of the ordinary - intriguing even - they are a pain in the rear to complete and I, for one, am in no hurry to do another.

CHAPTER 23

Beware, your shallow
digs will find you out

When the phone rings and the undertaker books me for a dig at either Long Bennington, Coddington, Leadenham, Norwell, Cottam, Flawborough, Barnby or Caythorpe, I instantly know that I'm in for a tough time. For most of my working life I have needed nothing more than my trusty pick, fork and shovel, but as the years pass I have become ever more reliant on my new friend, Mr Jack Hammer. There have been times when he has undoubtedly rescued the day and saved me both time and backbreaking toil.

Does this mean that as I get older I will purchase a mechanical digger? No, as I still believe that a grave should be of traditional shape and manually hand-dug. Whatever the conditions I've faced I have always endeavoured to make sure that the dig I'm completing is of adequate depth. At times this is easier said than done; it can be time-consuming and demoralising, but with patience, perseverance and sheer hard graft it is always achievable. There have been times when

I have struggled and even doubted my own ability to complete a task within a fixed time, but I have never failed to deliver.

For my own peace of mind, I do not want anyone coming along and reopening a grave that I originally dug, to find that there's barely enough room for a second interment. I'd rather eat my shovel than under-dig the grave!

Working in clay, stone or marl can be challenging enough, but it's the shaping of the head, shoulders and grave walls that can be time-consuming. Keeping the correct size and shape from start to finish is difficult. When working in sand and gravel you often end up slightly bigger at the bottom than at the top, which is fine providing the soft mixture can support its own weight – otherwise, it will collapse. In other material it's the opposite, often ending up smaller on the bottom than at the top which makes it harder to finally shape-up the dig. Over the years I have learned that on these types of digs it is always best to slightly over-dig the top, thereby allowing the grave walls to come in and resulting in a near-perfect finish.

There are a number of genuine reasons why a double-depth grave may end up a shallow dig. A wet spell and a high water table may ultimately force you to abandon a six-foot dig. When this happens, the neighbouring space is usually reserved for future use. Poor, unstable ground may cause a collapse, though in many cases this can be rectified and dealt with accordingly. The ground itself can halt proceedings as shale, stone and well-baked clay or marl can easily impede progress. Over the years I have learned not to take any-thing for granted and to be prepared for the unex-pected, as it's not only Mother Nature that can cause you grief. On my travels I have found brick walls, land drains, water pipes, sewer drains, brick vaults and even the odd cobbled floor.

When reopening a grave, you often expect to uncover the lid of the first coffin interred - but not at the shal-low depth of just 28inches. Initially I wasn't unduly concerned because the churchyard I was in was renowned for its high water table. With this in mind, I just presumed that the grave had originally been dug as a single and so had been mistakenly marked. This normally meant that the adjoining plot would have been reserved for future use. Unfortunately the funeral director told me that the information was correct and that it had been dug for two interments. My findings were promptly passed on to the family, though they themselves were undeterred and insisted that the burial must continue. In this type of situation there are a cou-ple of things you can do. The first is the old gravedig-ger's trick of raising the walk-boards some 6-8 inches, giving the illusion of a deeper-dug grave. Despite the fact that this could be done, the coffin would still only be a foot or so below the surface. With this in mind the undertaker and I decided that before backfilling the grave, I would wrap the coffin in thick, heavy-duty polythene. Spoil would then be placed around the outer edge, with an even layer spread thinly on top. Three concrete slabs would then be placed, thereby sealing it and preventing both the lid from collapsing or any nasty smells from escaping. One other tried and tested method is to wrap the coffin in polythene and then fill the grave to just six inches from the surface with concrete. Either way works well! At the time of the burial I was unaware that the gravedigger who had originally dug the grave was actually one of the pallbearers. He did not make himself known and was quick to make an exit.

CHAPTER 24

Floating coffin

When visiting out-of-the-way churchyards, it's not unusual to find that the grave I'm going to dig has not been marked. What is more worrying is when the churchwarden declares: 'What funeral? No-one's told me there's a burial here.' On one such occasion an unscheduled tea break was taken while an anxious churchwarden frantically ran around trying to clarify what, when and where. Eventually, after much confusion, he returned and a plot was chosen and finally I could begin.

It was to be a double-depth grave, but right from the start it was apparent that it had been dug before. This did not immediately concern me, as over the years many churchyards have been dug and re-dug. But, within a short time I had unearthed both a coffin and human remains, neither of which appeared to be that old. I couldn't now reach the churchwarden, so I telephoned the undertaker who was able to point me in the direction of someone who could help. On their arrival I explained the situation and for a moment they seemed clearly taken aback and at a loss as to quite what to do. According to the burial plan, the grave I had opened showed it to have been unused, but clearly that was not the case. It appeared that someone had forgotten to record the burial on the plan. Between us we examined the map of the churchyard and eventually decided on a new place to dig, so the other grave was abandoned and backfilled before starting all over again.

Digging was slow progress as the grey, potter's-type clay just glued itself to everything. It was strenuous, horrible stuff to work with as literally everything you touched was caked in clay. Keeping your footing while standing on the surrounding walk-boards was easier said than done, as the sodden earth made them extremely slippery and hazardous to work on. As with all clay-based digs, what I find typically frustrating is how it sticks to the heels of your boots and you're forever trying to scrape it off. It's so annoying! At a depth of 3ft 4ins I suddenly found myself in water and it was coming in fast. In fact I had never seen water rise so quickly, it was like running a bath. Without hiring a snorkel and flippers, a double-depth grave was out of the question and so I closed it down and left it until the day of the funeral.

On my return, I was somewhat surprised to find that there was only about 2ft of water in the grave. This was quickly pumped out, though it remained an ongoing task throughout. I tried to get a little more on the depth, but it was a no-win situation so I simply levelled off and dressed it ready for their arrival. Just minutes before they were due I again pumped out the grave and, in a bid to mask the rising tide, I threw in a generous amount of wood shavings. Unfortunately the hearse and cortege were running behind time and I was beginning to fret as the grave was filling up fast. To make things worse, when they did finally arrive and the coffin was interred, the mourners simply hung around conversing with each other. With every minute that passed I was becoming more worried that the coffin itself would float to the surface.

Finally, as the last mourner left, I quickly made my way to the grave. As I pulled out the webbings, the coffin simply bobbed about like a small boat. It may sound daft but I had to be careful while removing the straps as I feared it might capsize. When backfilling I had no choice but to stand directly on top of the coffin, weighing it down, while I shovelled in spoil on top. It was a delicate procedure as it was continually moving about; in effect I was coffin-surfing. If my colleague had been on hand to help, then our two weights combined would have been enough to hold it down, but mine alone was not.

I don't believe for one minute that the coffin would have actually floated to the top. Nevertheless the problem I had was that, although I placed the larger, heavier lumps of clay on the lid, I could not fully prevent spoil from falling around the edges which then pushed up the water level. It was a frustrating operation, but my perseverance finally paid off and thankfully no-one was any the wiser. Even when the turf was reinstated, it was so waterlogged that if anyone had stood directly on the grave they would have immediately sunk to their knees. I have dug many graves in clay land, but this one job certainly beat them all.

CHAPTER 25

Unknown danger

Prior to digging this grave, I had been forewarned to expect and prepare myself for a gruelling and strenuous challenge. Even the undertaker had suggested to allow plenty of time and strongly advised that I should take the demolition hammer and a sturdy crowbar as it would not be easy. A fellow gravedigger agreed. 'Rather you than me, expect shale and stone,' he said.

Friday, December 9th, 2005. A freezing cold start with a heavy frost and dense, freezing fog, it was not ideal for travelling. Although the burial was not until the Monday, I had allowed the two of us a full day's digging for what was initially only a single-depth grave. Once on site I couldn't find a grave marker and, after completing an extensive search, I contacted the undertaker. Three long hours passed before the undertaker was finally able to contact someone and, even then, we had to go and pick them up. Armed with a giant plan of the cemetery, my colleague and I watched in astonishment as this somewhat eccentric woman wandered aimlessly around the cemetery.

She eventually admitted that she was at a total loss as to what she was doing. I offered to help and even located a vacant plot near to other newly-dug graves, but she was having none of it. Her indecisiveness eventually confused both my colleague and I so much that we went and sat in the van, leaving her to it. After a further 20 minutes she finally concluded that the plot I had originally chosen would in fact be the best one to use. Hooray!

With the shape cut and the turf removed, the dig went straight into stone though it turned out to be just a thin top layer. Underneath this was bronze-coloured clay which carved out with relative ease, though from 2ft onwards it was a very different story. From here on it was a sandstone mixture, though to be fair it broke up nicely with the demolition hammer. It was at this point that a local farmer spotted us toiling away and came over for a chat. He told us that his father, who himself had died only a few days before, had been the cemetery's gravedigger for many years. Looking down into the grave, he said, 'Looks like you've been quite lucky. It's terrible, dire digging here and my father had many a nightmare.

'Is it a single or a double?' he asked. 'It's just a single,' I replied. He nodded his head and added, 'Good! If it was a double then I was going to warn you of what may lie beneath.' Intrigued by his comment, I asked, 'Why?' He replied, 'I guess no-one has told you. I don't wish to alarm you, but on one occasion while digging a double-depth grave my father - using a metal crowbar to remove huge lumps of stone - suddenly lost it through a gaping hole that appeared. While peering through the void below him, he was even more shocked to discover a fast-running, underground stream. He honestly believed that if he had fallen through, he would surely have been trapped and may even have been swept away.' With that bombshell dropped, I called a tea break and swiftly climbed out.

What an unnerving thought; it's bad enough when a coffin collapses under your weight, but just the thought of falling into a dark, underground cavern, well, it sent shivers down my spine. Fortunately my dig revealed no nasty, hidden surprises and by mid-afternoon we were happily on our way home. As yet I've never been called upon to dig there again, but if I am I will be sure to keep my wits about me.

CHAPTER 26

All or nothing

The old timers would often grumble that if there had not been a long lasting cold snap with snow and frost by Christmas, then for certain the New Year would start busy. They would often say, 'A green Christmas, a packed (or fat) churchyard.' For the most part winter is my busiest time, but to cover five interments on one day in three different locations is no easy feat. With Christmas looming, and fully aware of the workload ahead, my colleague and I began digging out two new double-depth graves in Newark Cemetery. Ideally I would have liked to have completed them both, but I was restricted to just how much I could do as it was not the done thing to leave spoil covering any other graves, especially at this time of year.

December 27th – After a short break it was back to it and the weather had turned and snow was in the air. The sudden change was a cruel shock to the system. Thankfully my one job of the day was in a village just a few miles away from home. It was a typical clay dig, great for shaping but tough all the same. Oddly the land in this churchyard is constantly on the move, which I'm told has something to do with gravel pits and underground streams. This effectively rules out any double-depth digs, as they not only flood but the moving earth causes collapse. At 3ft6 I was in water; there was no point in finishing the job as it had to stand a couple of nights, so I closed it down.

December 28th – The bitter wind that had annoyed me the day before had thankfully dropped, though in its place lay a generous covering of snow. With a hectic day ahead I called in extra help, which included my two brothers and Alison (now my wife), who I might say is extremely handy with a shovel. That day's first call was Newark Cemetery where I had to finish the two I had previously started before Christmas. I then had to reopen another grave, before finally returning to my home village of Swinderby to dig a new single grave. Many hands make light work and by 3pm my colleagues and I were at my house enjoying a warming brew, before tackling the final job of the day. The digging in Swinderby churchyard is variable to say the least. It can be awkward, it can be soft, but on the whole it is a sand, gravel and clay mixture which is hampered by a high water table. The dazzling white snow illuminated the churchyard, keeping dusk at bay just long enough for me to almost complete the dig. On the downside, thick freezing fog had descended, cutting visibility down to well under 50 yards. It was not wise to travel and, as my brother Dave lived in Derbyshire, he sensibly decided to stay over rather than risk a dicey drive home then have to repeat the journey the following day.

Thursday, December 29th – With five burials on my mind I was up early, and by break of light Dave and I were in

Swinderby churchyard where the first job was to pump out the grave. Remarkably it had not collapsed, though I was not entirely convinced it would remain that way. As the two village burials at Swinderby and Thorpe on the Hill were only a stone's throw apart, I chose to leave the backfilling to my brothers, Paul and Dave. My wife then assisted me while I sorted out the three remaining burials at Newark Cemetery. If all went to plan, by the time of the last – and by far the biggest - interment (3pm), we'd all be in the same place (Newark) and could complete the task with comparative ease.

Although everything went accordingly, it had been a long and tiring couple of days with a tight schedule and a lot of running around. The weather had been foul and far from kind, but more importantly deadlines had been met and I was pleased. Five hours, five funerals, three different locations; in truth it had stretched me to my limit and I could not have pulled it off without help. Many years before I had backfilled four burials in one afternoon, but at least they had been in the same cemetery. Currently, 2005 still remains my busiest year ever, with a total of 204 graves being dug.

CHAPTER 27

Strange request

Late one Sunday evening there was a sudden unexpected knock at my door. It was my next door neighbour with a somewhat odd request. She said, 'I'm sorry to bother you at this late hour. This is going to sound extremely bizarre, but a friend of mine wondered if you would be prepared to exhume their pet dog. She would understand if you would prefer not to, it's just that they are moving house and they don't want to leave their dog behind, and her husband can't face doing it.' I must admit I was somewhat taken aback at being asked to undertake such an unusual job, but nevertheless I agreed.

It was only later, when I'd had time to think it over, that I realised the unpleasantness of the task ahead. Apparently the dog - a lurcher - had died six weeks previously and been buried in the garden in a shallow grave, wrapped in a duvet. In the weeks following we'd had both heavy rain and snow, which had left the land extremely boggy. It did not bode well! Wet and whiffy, that's how I assumed the job would be and, with this in mind, I went totally prepared. On site I carefully began to dig down and within minutes I had found and unearthed the duvet in which the dog was wrapped. By chance, the area in which the dog had been buried had been sheltered from the elements and so had remained relatively dry. Unfortunately, as soon as it was disturbed, it began to smell. Once fully uncovered, the dog's remains were simply lifted out and immediately placed into a thick polythene bag, which was then sealed and placed in the boot of the owner's car. From there the family had arranged for their much-loved pet to be cremated. To finish, I spread a handful of quicklime both in and around the burial site, before simply backfilling and making tidy.

Nowadays vets wisely advise you not to bury your pets in the garden as, unlike in years gone by, people are quick to move on and the thought of leaving a cherished family pet behind can be quite upsetting. When my dog died, I had her cremated so when I moved house she came with me. She now sits quietly in one corner of the room and when I die I will have her interred with me.

CHAPTER 28

A long wait

I had always been hopeful that one day I would get the opportunity to reopen the first grave I'd dug. All the same, I had not contemplated having to wait a quarter-of-a-century. My memory of that Tuesday in May 1982 is still vividly clear. I was a young 18-year-old lad who, as my colleagues pointed out, had not yet completed a proper day's hard graft. I was bursting with energy and eager to get stuck in. I remember being told not to be so hasty, or I would be worn out before I got started. Furthermore, I was repeatedly told to listen to my colleague, keep the shape true and the grave walls straight because the coffin was not made to fit the shape of my dig.

I was always aware that the likelihood of me reopening this grave was high, but it had been a long time coming. I was absorbed by the whole concept, though I was a bit worried that the dig would be shaped like a dog's hind leg, which would have embarrassed me slightly. I had decided beforehand that I was not going to needlessly spoil the dig by fixing shoring, though to be fair in the area it was in it was unlikely to collapse. I purposely did not alter or reshape the grave in any way or form, as I just wanted to follow the original shape in full. The hard work had been done the first time around and, unlike then when it took all of one day to complete, this was finished with ease in less than three hours. Eager to inspect my original handiwork I climbed out and proceeded to give it a good coat of looking-at.

My colleague, ever the joker, also gave it the once-over before commenting, 'Hmm, it's a bit skew-whiff on one side and one shoulder is slightly lower than the other, but it'll pass.' I knew he was pulling my leg but I still could have kicked him. I had waited a long time to do this and, if I'm honest, I was more than pleased with the end result. It was over regulation depth and for a first dig I was impressed with how well-shaped it actually was. Compared to a modern-day dig, it was small and close-fitting, a neat job just like they should be. The only drawback was that I now had to spoil it by both widening and lengthening it because it wasn't big enough. That was like defacing an original piece of art, but it was only out of necessity that I did it.

I was thrilled that I had got to reopen my first ever dig and was happily satisfied that it wasn't shaped like a 50 pence piece or even a banana.

CHAPTER 29

A horrible winter's day

'More rain, more rest,' that's what old timer, Ted Sumner, used to say and in days gone by that was exactly how it was. It was known as wet time and every now and then, if it had not cleared by lunch, we'd be sent home but would have to make up the hours by working a Saturday morning. Nowadays this is no longer the case. Forget the difficult digs and the short winter days, if the elements are against you then you're in for a miserable time. No, a gravedigger's life is not always a happy one and every so often I curse and think to myself, 'Ian, you must be mad!'

It's not often that I'm asked to dig a grave outside my normal working area, but every once in a while a request is made. In a village near Rutland Water - the furthest I have travelled - I was asked to dig a single-depth grave. The cemetery was situated on the outskirts of the village. It was remote,and barren. Surrounding me on three sides were steep, rolling hills while the fourth side was entirely flat, allowing you to see for miles and miles. I would imagine that during the summer months it would have been a beautiful, picturesque place but at the end of

January, with snow on the ground and a bitter wind blowing a chill factor of minus 13, it was a very, very different story.

Prior to starting out, I had been warned that it would not be an easy dig as it was stony ground and, once past the thin layer of turf, it was like trying to dig through a road. Shovel, fork and pick were all but useless and, although the jack-hammer did loosen it, it struggled because the stones got bigger the deeper I went. Up until lunch the weather had been fairly kind but then it suddenly changed with a vengeance. Wind, rain, sleet and finally heavy driving snow pounded us for over four hours. Oddly, if you looked to the hills you could see the weather as it rapidly closed in. It was an awesome sight as the peaks suddenly changed from green to white, and within a matter of minutes it totally engulfed us.

I had no choice but to continue working as I had only allowed myself one full day for digging. However, my colleague and I were struggling as the severe weather began to take its toll. It was so wet and icy that there was a real danger that one of us might get electrocuted, so as a precaution I stopped using the jack-hammer. Fortunately I was able to shield the generator and keep it running just so we could warm our hands from the heat of the exhaust. By late afternoon the skies had cleared, but the wind increased and the temperature plummeted. Neither my colleague nor I could remember a time when we had ever felt so cold. We were both soaked to the skin and at one point I couldn't stop myself from shivering. My hands were so numb that I couldn't even hold my shovel.

Nevertheless, I was determined to get finished and by dusk we had virtually completed the dig. Worn out and chilled to the core, sitting in wet clothes with the heater at full blast did nothing to raise morale and, with over 30 miles to travel, I can honestly say it was basically a cheerless and uncomfortable journey home. I do not recall my colleague and I engaging in any conversation at all. I know my thoughts were on a hot bath, dry clothes, a warming fire and a hearty meal, and I'm guessing my colleague was thinking the same.

On the day of the funeral we returned to site, though the weather was no better. I managed to scrape out a few more inches in depth, before dressing the grave and clearing a pathway for pallbearers and mourners to walk on. Regrettably, what I had neglected to do on the day of digging was to throw a spare tarpaulin over the spoil heap and, as a result, it had frozen solid. A couple of days of heavy frosts had bonded the entire heap together and it was so tightly-knitted that for the first time in years I had to use a pick to break it up before shovelling it back in. I have had many an unpleasant dig, but without doubt this was the coldest, wettest and most miserable of jobs that I can ever remember doing.

Chapter 30

Should we cancel the funeral?

If it's not the winter weather causing the gravedigger problems, then it's unseasonable summer storms which wreak havoc and cause flash flooding and collapse. The freak storms of May and June 2007 had left the land saturated, making it heavy, muddy and unstable and causing grave after grave to cave in. The spoil just could not support its own weight and even fixing extra shoring did not prevent it from giving way. For a time it was a real problem, so much so that it very nearly caused the cancellation of a funeral just hours before it was due.

Although the grave had been adequately shored, it had collapsed. In addition to this, the headstone on the neighbouring grave, on the side that had fallen in, was now dangerously suspended in mid-air and causing me great concern. The headstone and its base had toppled to one side and there was a high risk that it might fall into the open grave below. It was a hefty stone and the only thing supporting it was the shoring itself, and even this was perilously close to giving way. With less than five hours before the burial, I met the undertaker and a council representative to discuss what we should do.

My immediate priority was to make the headstone safe, though securing it with upright supports and ropes was rife with problems, as the surrounding ground was itself unstable and so there was nothing secure to anchor it to. Secondly, I could try to fix more shoring and then backfill the space beside, behind and underneath. But to do this would have meant removing shoring already fixed, thereby readjusting it before re-fixing it back into place. As the shoring was the only thing supporting the headstone and the remaining grave wall, I was not prepared to take that chance. If the headstone had fallen and ended up in the bottom of the grave, retrieving it would not have been easy. The third option, and my preference, was for a stonemason to remove the headstone and re-fix it after the funeral, though this idea was not even considered. As a result, neither I nor the undertaker could put forward a way to immediately resolve the situation, as there was no right or wrong way of dealing with it.

On this basis the council representative declared that, on Health and Safety grounds, the funeral should be cancelled until further notice. Nobody wanted this, especially the disgruntled undertaker who said, 'That's not an option, it's too late to postpone. The cortege is coming from over 50 miles away and up to 400 mourners are expected to attend.' But the council woman's reply was blunt and direct, as she declared: 'If I feel it's unsafe to continue, then I have no alternative but to cancel the funeral and this I am more than prepared to do,' It was all very dramatic but, after calmly talking it through, it was agreed that the funeral would be allowed to go ahead with certain conditions.

The immediate area on three sides of the grave must be cordoned off to keep mourners at a safe distance. Extra walk-boards would be placed around the immediate area, and during the funeral only the undertaker and his pallbearers would be allowed to approach the grave. Only once the coffin had been safely interred would the immediate family be allowed to pay their final respects. This was mutually agreed, though it all hung in the balance and depended on whether or not the headstone and grave remained standing. It was fingers crossed!

By the time the funeral arrived the skies had darkened and the heavens had opened. The rain was relentless. Worryingly, neither the immediate family nor the accompanying mourners took heed of the undertaker's advice and between them removed all safety barriers so that they could get as close as they could. There was nothing I or anyone else could do but look on and hope that no-one would come to any harm. Thankfully the funeral did pass without incident.

At graveside it was noticeable that the headstone had dropped further. It was now totally unsupported and on the brink of plummeting below. What was needed was a nifty backfill, though that was easier said than done because the spoil had to be wheelbarrowed some 50ft before being tipped into the grave. The heavy rain had turned the sand and gravel mixture to sludge; it was like shovelling wet cement. Once I'd reached the height of the shoring, I quickly released the screw-jacks, removed the woods and stood clear. Barrow by barrow I continued to cram the sodden earth under and around the headstone. I was aware that this would only be a quick temporary fix and, once the ground had settled, the headstone and base would be in need of some serious attention. A few weeks later the headstone was indeed reset at no cost to the family.

CHAPTER 31

Strange people

Wad Man Morris

Wad Man Morris, or 'Mo' as he was better known, was not a regular visitor to the cemetery but every now and then he would call in just to catch up with the old timers. Now Mo thought himself a bit of a geezer, a real-life Del Boy, who dressed himself not too dissimilar to George Cole's character in the TV series, *Minder*. He had both the charisma and personality, and he could certainly talk you out of your last pound.

He would openly boast about his trips abroad and repeatedly tell us about the glorious and glamorous life he lived in his second home in Tenerife. He once said to me, 'You're young. Take a chance, trust me and let me invest your money in property abroad. You won't be sorry for I'll make you rich.' Fortunately I never fell for it. Whenever Mo would speak to you, he had a habit of removing his wallet from his inside jacket pocket and, as he talked, he would continually be waving it in front of your face. You couldn't fail to notice nor be impressed as it was a very, very fat wallet indeed.

However, things are not always what they seem. On one occasion Mo accidentally dropped his wallet and, as a colleague bent down to pick it up, out rolled what appeared to be a large wad of cash. As he handed it to Mo, we could all see that it was in fact a cut-to-size bundle of newspaper, wrapped on the outside with one solitary £20 note. Mo had been sussed and with that he quickly made his excuses and left. To this day we have never seen him again.

Scary Dawn

Dawn was a formidable woman and whenever she made an appearance all staff, no matter what they were doing, would simply dive for cover. I'm not joking when I say that she was built like a Russian shot-putter, as she was extremely masculine. Moustache, beard, hairy legs, she was no beauty queen and definitely not the type to be messed with. I recall one afternoon just after lunch, we were all sitting in the old donkey stable waiting for a storm to pass when in walked Dawn. She immediately made a beeline for one of my older colleagues and asked, 'Got any spare bacca, mate?' With that, she proceeded to make herself at home by nestling herself between him and a fellow workmate. No-one dared to look at her or engage her in conversation, and as soon as the storm passed, out we scarpered. Unfortunately, our older colleague was not as quick on his feet and Dawn got up and immediately closed and bolted the stable door from the inside.

We all fell about laughing, as we could only imagine what she was doing to our poor colleague. Minutes later, the stable door opened and out they came. Dawn stomped off in one direction while our traumatised colleague came towards us. 'I'm all of a jitter,' he announced. 'I don't half need a smoke,' he said, sitting himself down. Eventually our teasing stopped and we got around to asking him what had happened.

He said, 'She came on a bit strong. She wouldn't let me out until I promised that I would get her a job and she's coming back tomorrow to find out when she starts.' The following day he, like the rest of us, was in constant fear of her arrival but happily she never turned up. Though if our colleague thought for one minute that he had got away with it, then he was sadly mistaken. The following day on return from lunch, who should we find waiting by the old donkey stable but Dawn. 'Alright, Mister,' she said. 'It's okay, I don't need the job any more, as I'm going to be a trucker's mate.' My colleague was so relieved; as for Dawn, she never bothered us again.

Tramp Man

From where he came and eventually where he went, we would never know, because Tramp Man never spoke to either me nor my colleagues. But, for a few weeks during one summer, he could be found sleeping rough under the bushes and trees at Newark Cemetery. He was never once a nuisance and, surprisingly, always tidied up after himself. When mowing the grass you'd simply mow around him, and it never appeared to wake him up.

One morning I arrived at work to find two of my colleagues wandering around the outside of the cemetery's chapel. 'What's up?' I asked, to which they replied,

'The door key is missing and the chapel door was open, but no-one's about and nothing is missing.' A further search revealed nothing, but the missing key was causing concern. Back then, once the chapel door was locked the key was hidden under a pile of roof tiles which only the staff knew about. It was obvious that someone had seen us lock up and hide the key. At tea break we all returned to the mess-room, which at that time was in part of the cemetery chapel.

We had literally just sat down when a colleague abruptly jumped up out of his seat and pointed in the direction of a pile of green dressing mats. In a low voice, he told us all, 'I swear that I've just seen that pile of green sheets move.' We all got up to take a closer look. 'See! There it is again, they did move!' Immediately another of my workmates grabbed a brush and began to lift up the sheets one at a time with the shaft end. Before he could move them all, out sprang Tramp Man who quickly dashed out of the door and ran off up the main drive. There had been a thunderstorm the previous evening and so he must have caught sight of us hiding the key and had let himself in to take shelter. His untimely departure had half-frightened us all to death, but on a plus note at least we had recovered the key.

Old Waldo

Walter (Waldo) was a fellow colleague, an old timer who'd worked at the cemetery for a good 20 years. My first encounter with him is one I won't forget, as I'd just walked into the chapel to find a work experience lad getting up off the floor, in tears and holding his nose. It emerged that this lad had trapped Walter's hand in the door and in response the older man had turned round and punched him directly on the nose, sending him crashing to the floor. The lad went crying to the cemetery superintendent, who simply told him to grow up.

Now old boy Walter was more or less deaf which meant communicating with him was extremely difficult, so much so that only Ted could seemingly get through to him. Even then, Ted would only get a responsive smile, followed by an acknowledging, 'Oooh aargh.' Often we would unashamedly play on this and would ask him things like, 'Have you farted, Walter?' to which he'd reply, 'Oooh aargh', much to our amusement.

At home Walter would wear a hearing aid, but it was only after much persuasion from Ted that he began to wear it at work. But our schoolboy behaviour soon put paid to that when a workmate who was chatting to him suddenly stopped talking, but continued to mouth the words. Walter, thinking that his hearing aid had packed up, began fiddling with the volume switch. When it was fully turned up, my colleague continued with the conversation but at a much higher level. This, coupled with a high-pitched, feed-back squeal, just about shattered what remained of poor Walter's eardrums and he completely lost his temper. I distinctly recall him grabbing hold of a sweeping brush and giving chase to my colleague, shouting: 'Come here, you little bugger! I'm going to teach you a lesson you won't forget.' He never did wear his hearing aid to work again.

Jack Frost

Jack Frost was, without doubt, a grumpy old man who never had a good word to say about anything or anyone.

He would visit and tend to his wife's grave at least four times a week, bringing fresh flowers and mowing the grass. The grave was immaculate, meticulously kept and definitely a credit to him. He would stand for hours beside the headstone and if anyone came close to walking near to his plot, he would frantically wave his walking stick at them.

One autumn during leaf fall, after a hard night's frost, a workmate unintentionally walked across the grave. A week later and his footprints could be seen burnt into the turf, scorching the grass and leaving a set of black footmarks. On seeing the damage, the old man went berserk and immediately began tracking us down. One by one he threatened us all, stating that when he found out who was responsible he would kill the guilty culprit. Harsh words indeed. He even requested that the superintendent match the footprints to those of his staff's workboots. He raged for months afterwards, but never did find out who had walked across the grave. From that moment onwards, nobody went within ten feet of it.

Dumber and Dumber

Without any doubt, the daftest two questions I have ever been asked have come from schoolkids. One asked me, 'How deep is a six-foot grave?' I looked at him gone out and said, 'About five foot twelve inches should do it.' Another one asked, 'How deep is that grave, Mister?' I replied, 'It's six foot, two inches.' He then said, 'Wow! My mate's 16 years old and seven foot tall, that grave is deeper than he is high.' There was no answer to that!

Chapter 32

Milestone

Thursday, July 5, 2007 –I reached another milestone in my career when I completed my 3,000th hand-dug grave and it was one I am not likely to forget in a hurry. After completing an early afternoon's backfill at Balderton Cemetery, my colleague and I were on the road and outward-bound, heading for the village of Caythorpe. On our arrival I was left scratching my head, because although we looked for the village churchyard we could not for the life of us locate one.

After an unsuccessful search I thought it best to ask a villager, but my request was met with nothing but hilarity. The man simply fell about laughing, before stating: 'There's no church or burial ground here. My guess is that you're in the wrong county altogether.' Feeling more than a little stupid, I telephoned the undertaker who himself thought it rather funny before confirming that, yes, the burial was indeed in Caythorpe, Lincolnshire and not - as I swear I had been told – in Caythorpe, Nottinghamshire. Whoops!

Just to make life more interesting, on our return journey we were hotly pursued by a bank of cloud, both dark and grey, and within minutes of reaching the correct destination it literally hammered it down with rain. For three uncomfortable hours my colleague and I persevered until finally we could take no more. The digging was awful, as it was all stone. The best description I could give is that it was like standing on top of a stone-built wall and dismantling it layer by layer, piece by piece. It was extremely frustrating because you seemingly got nowhere fast.

When I returned the next morning I was pleasantly surprised to find that the dig was actually deeper than I had initially believed it was. On the downside, it was now standing in 18 inches of water although this was quickly pumped out. The grave was sufficiently deep enough, but for my own peace of mind I picked up where I left off, eager to scrape out a few more inches. But it was a hopeless task, as each stone I removed simply let more water in. The grave had to be continually pumped out right up until the pallbearers arrived.

As I masked the bottom with wood shavings, one bearer asked, 'How come the water is running uphill and not down?' For a brief moment, and in silent wonderment, we all stared into the grave but there was no time to evaluate the reason as the cortege had arrived. Sat in the van, my colleague asked again, 'Why was the water running uphill?' I shrugged my shoulders and said, 'That's one of life's little mysteries.'

August 2009 - As I come to the end of writing this book, I'll be entering my 28th year as a gravedigger. To date I have hand-dug 3,380 graves and have dug in 107 different locations across Nottinghamshire and Lincolnshire.

I recently calculated that I have dug 1,954 single-depth graves (4ft6), 1,335 double-depth (6ft), 89 trebles and two at 9ft. In effect, this approximately relates to me having dug one average size grave, measuring 7ft long by 19inches (Head), 19inches (Foot) and 28inches (Shoulders), to a depth of 17,488 ft. Astonishingly, this turns out to be over three-and-a-quarter miles deep! I dare not contemplate just how much spoil I have handballed over the years, though it must be in the region of 9–10,000 tons - that's a lot of wheelbarrows!

The End

www.ingramcontent.com/pod-product-compliance
Lightning Source LLC
Chambersburg PA
CBHW051817040426
42446CB00007B/709